DIRECTOR´S

Notebook

Story Film House Books:
DIRECTORS NOTEBOOK V2 UPDATED 2018

Published by Story Film House™
Story Film House (Bogota - Colombia)
Calle 134 59A-81 of 607 T2.
Story Film House (Los Angeles -USA) (323) 7459735

Printed in USA. / Impreso en USA
by Created Space.
First edition Published by Story Film House.
www.StoryFilmHouse.com / www.CinemaNotebooks.com

DIRECTED BY

CONTACT NUMBER

SPECIAL INFO

HOW TO USE THE DIRECTOR'S NOTEBOOK

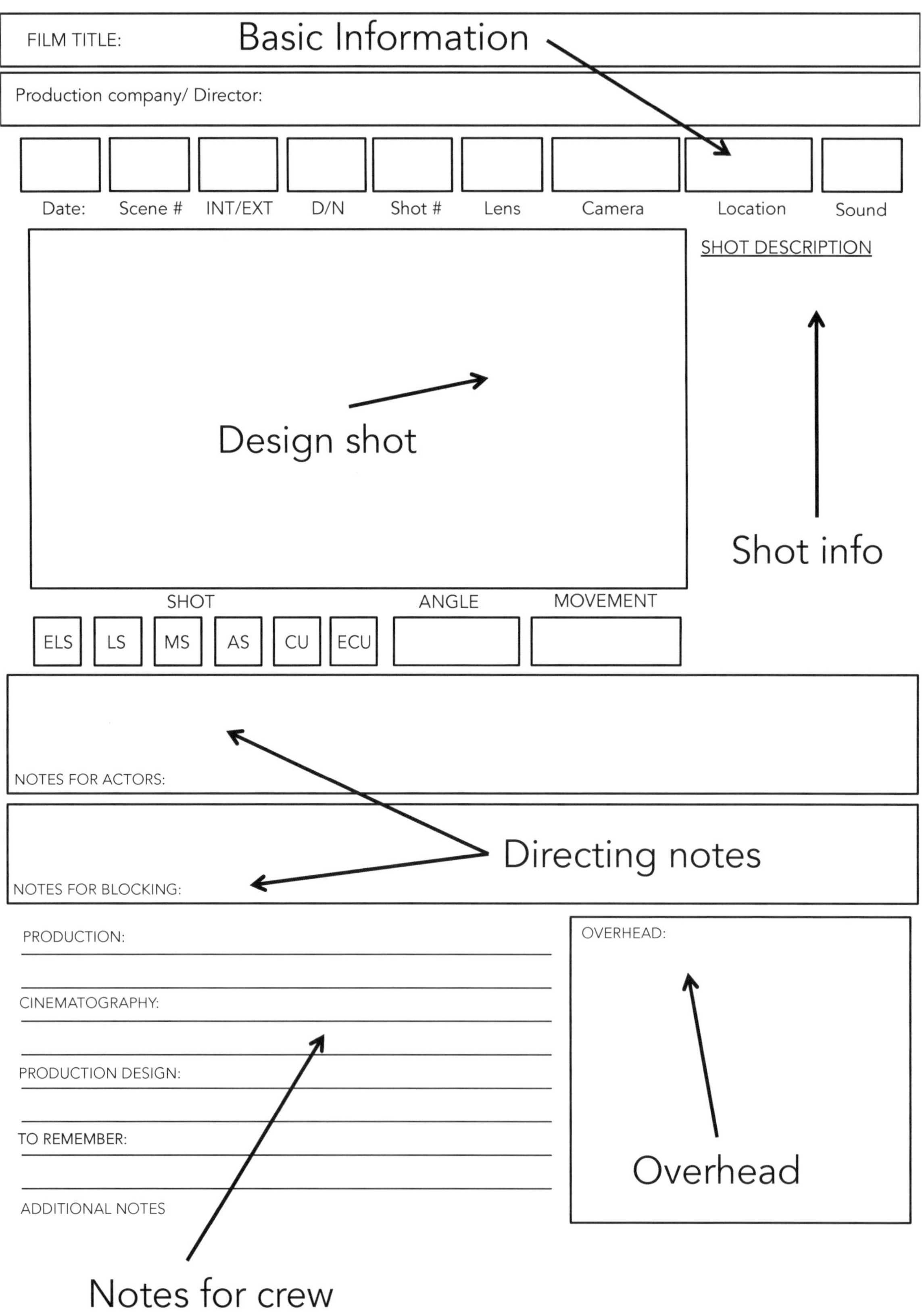

FILM TITLE:

Production company/ Director:

Date:	Scene #	INT/EXT	D/N	Shot #	Lens	Camera	Location	Sound

SHOT DESCRIPTION

SHOT

ELS LS MS AS CU ECU

ANGLE

MOVEMENT

NOTES FOR ACTORS:

NOTES FOR BLOCKING.

PRODUCTION:

CINEMATOGRAPHY:

PRODUCTION DESIGN:

TO REMEMBER:

ADDITIONAL NOTES

OVERHEAD:

FILM TITLE:

Production company/ Director:

Date:	Scene #	INT/EXT	D/N	Shot #	Lens	Camera	Location	Sound

SHOT DESCRIPTION

SHOT: ELS | LS | MS | AS | CU | ECU

ANGLE

MOVEMENT

NOTES FOR ACTORS:

NOTES FOR BLOCKING:

PRODUCTION:

CINEMATOGRAPHY:

PRODUCTION DESIGN:

TO REMEMBER:

ADDITIONAL NOTES

OVERHEAD:

FILM TITLE:

Production company/ Director:

Date:	Scene #	INT/EXT	D/N	Shot #	Lens	Camera	Location	Sound

SHOT DESCRIPTION

SHOT

ELS LS MS AS CU ECU

ANGLE

MOVEMENT

NOTES FOR ACTORS:

NOTES FOR BLOCKING:

PRODUCTION:

CINEMATOGRAPHY:

PRODUCTION DESIGN:

TO REMEMBER:

ADDITIONAL NOTES

OVERHEAD:

FILM TITLE:

Production company/ Director:

Date:	Scene #	INT/EXT	D/N	Shot #	Lens	Camera	Location	Sound

SHOT DESCRIPTION

SHOT

ELS LS MS AS CU ECU

ANGLE

MOVEMENT

NOTES FOR ACTORS:

NOTES FOR BLOCKING:

PRODUCTION:

CINEMATOGRAPHY:

PRODUCTION DESIGN:

TO REMEMBER:

ADDITIONAL NOTES

OVERHEAD:

FILM TITLE:

Production company/ Director:

Date:	Scene #	INT/EXT	D/N	Shot #	Lens	Camera	Location	Sound

SHOT DESCRIPTION

SHOT

ELS LS MS AS CU ECU

ANGLE

MOVEMENT

NOTES FOR ACTORS:

NOTES FOR BLOCKING:

PRODUCTION:

CINEMATOGRAPHY:

PRODUCTION DESIGN:

TO REMEMBER:

ADDITIONAL NOTES

OVERHEAD:

FILM TITLE:

Production company/ Director:

Date:	Scene #	INT/EXT	D/N	Shot #	Lens	Camera	Location	Sound

SHOT DESCRIPTION

SHOT

ELS LS MS AS CU ECU

ANGLE

MOVEMENT

NOTES FOR ACTORS:

NOTES FOR BLOCKING:

PRODUCTION:

CINEMATOGRAPHY:

PRODUCTION DESIGN:

TO REMEMBER:

ADDITIONAL NOTES

OVERHEAD:

FILM TITLE:

Production company/ Director:

Date:	Scene #	INT/EXT	D/N	Shot #	Lens	Camera	Location	Sound

SHOT DESCRIPTION

SHOT

ELS LS MS AS CU ECU

ANGLE

MOVEMENT

NOTES FOR ACTORS:

NOTES FOR BLOCKING:

PRODUCTION:

CINEMATOGRAPHY:

PRODUCTION DESIGN:

TO REMEMBER:

ADDITIONAL NOTES

OVERHEAD:

FILM TITLE:

Production company/ Director:

Date: | Scene # | INT/EXT | D/N | Shot # | Lens | Camera | Location | Sound

SHOT DESCRIPTION

SHOT

ELS | LS | MS | AS | CU | ECU

ANGLE

MOVEMENT

NOTES FOR ACTORS:

NOTES FOR BLOCKING:

PRODUCTION:

CINEMATOGRAPHY:

PRODUCTION DESIGN:

TO REMEMBER:

ADDITIONAL NOTES

OVERHEAD:

FILM TITLE:

Production company/ Director:

Date:	Scene #	INT/EXT	D/N	Shot #	Lens	Camera	Location	Sound

SHOT DESCRIPTION

SHOT

ELS LS MS AS CU ECU

ANGLE

MOVEMENT

NOTES FOR ACTORS:

NOTES FOR BLOCKING:

PRODUCTION:

CINEMATOGRAPHY:

PRODUCTION DESIGN:

TO REMEMBER:

ADDITIONAL NOTES

OVERHEAD:

FILM TITLE:

Production company/ Director:

Date:	Scene #	INT/EXT	D/N	Shot #	Lens	Camera	Location	Sound

SHOT DESCRIPTION

SHOT

ELS LS MS AS CU ECU

ANGLE

MOVEMENT

NOTES FOR ACTORS:

NOTES FOR BLOCKING:

PRODUCTION:

CINEMATOGRAPHY:

PRODUCTION DESIGN:

TO REMEMBER:

ADDITIONAL NOTES

OVERHEAD:

FILM TITLE:

Production company/ Director:

Date:	Scene #	INT/EXT	D/N	Shot #	Lens	Camera	Location	Sound

SHOT DESCRIPTION

SHOT

ELS LS MS AS CU ECU

ANGLE

MOVEMENT

NOTES FOR ACTORS:

NOTES FOR BLOCKING:

PRODUCTION:

CINEMATOGRAPHY:

PRODUCTION DESIGN:

TO REMEMBER:

ADDITIONAL NOTES

OVERHEAD:

FILM TITLE:

Production company/ Director:

Date:	Scene #	INT/EXT	D/N	Shot #	Lens	Camera	Location	Sound

SHOT DESCRIPTION

SHOT

ELS | LS | MS | AS | CU | ECU

ANGLE

MOVEMENT

NOTES FOR ACTORS:

NOTES FOR BLOCKING:

PRODUCTION:

CINEMATOGRAPHY:

PRODUCTION DESIGN:

TO REMEMBER:

ADDITIONAL NOTES

OVERHEAD:

FILM TITLE:

Production company/ Director:

Date:	Scene #	INT/EXT	D/N	Shot #	Lens	Camera	Location	Sound

SHOT DESCRIPTION

SHOT

ELS LS MS AS CU ECU

ANGLE

MOVEMENT

NOTES FOR ACTORS:

NOTES FOR BLOCKING:

PRODUCTION:

CINEMATOGRAPHY:

PRODUCTION DESIGN:

TO REMEMBER:

ADDITIONAL NOTES

OVERHEAD:

FILM TITLE:

Production company/ Director:

Date:	Scene #	INT/EXT	D/N	Shot #	Lens	Camera	Location	Sound

SHOT DESCRIPTION

SHOT

ELS LS MS AS CU ECU

ANGLE

MOVEMENT

NOTES FOR ACTORS:

NOTES FOR BLOCKING:

PRODUCTION:

CINEMATOGRAPHY:

PRODUCTION DESIGN:

TO REMEMBER:

ADDITIONAL NOTES

OVERHEAD:

FILM TITLE:

Production company/ Director:

Date:	Scene #	INT/EXT	D/N	Shot #	Lens	Camera	Location	Sound

SHOT DESCRIPTION

SHOT

ELS LS MS AS CU ECU

ANGLE

MOVEMENT

NOTES FOR ACTORS:

NOTES FOR BLOCKING:

PRODUCTION:

CINEMATOGRAPHY:

PRODUCTION DESIGN:

TO REMEMBER:

ADDITIONAL NOTES

OVERHEAD:

FILM TITLE:

Production company/ Director:

Date:	Scene #	INT/EXT	D/N	Shot #	Lens	Camera	Location	Sound

SHOT DESCRIPTION

SHOT

ELS LS MS AS CU ECU

ANGLE

MOVEMENT

NOTES FOR ACTORS:

NOTES FOR BLOCKING:

PRODUCTION:

CINEMATOGRAPHY:

PRODUCTION DESIGN:

TO REMEMBER:

ADDITIONAL NOTES

OVERHEAD:

FILM TITLE:

Production company/ Director:

Date:	Scene #	INT/EXT	D/N	Shot #	Lens	Camera	Location	Sound

SHOT DESCRIPTION

SHOT

ELS LS MS AS CU ECU

ANGLE

MOVEMENT

NOTES FOR ACTORS:

NOTES FOR BLOCKING:

PRODUCTION:

CINEMATOGRAPHY:

PRODUCTION DESIGN:

TO REMEMBER:

ADDITIONAL NOTES

OVERHEAD:

FILM TITLE:

Production company/ Director:

Date:	Scene #	INT/EXT	D/N	Shot #	Lens	Camera	Location	Sound

SHOT DESCRIPTION

SHOT: ELS | LS | MS | AS | CU | ECU

ANGLE

MOVEMENT

NOTES FOR ACTORS:

NOTES FOR BLOCKING:

PRODUCTION:

CINEMATOGRAPHY:

PRODUCTION DESIGN:

TO REMEMBER:

ADDITIONAL NOTES

OVERHEAD:

FILM TITLE:

Production company/ Director:

Date:	Scene #	INT/EXT	D/N	Shot #	Lens	Camera	Location	Sound

SHOT DESCRIPTION

SHOT

ELS LS MS AS CU ECU

ANGLE

MOVEMENT

NOTES FOR ACTORS:

NOTES FOR BLOCKING:

PRODUCTION:

CINEMATOGRAPHY:

PRODUCTION DESIGN:

TO REMEMBER:

ADDITIONAL NOTES

OVERHEAD:

FILM TITLE:

Production company/ Director:

Date:	Scene #	INT/EXT	D/N	Shot #	Lens	Camera	Location	Sound

SHOT DESCRIPTION

SHOT

ELS LS MS AS CU ECU

ANGLE

MOVEMENT

NOTES FOR ACTORS:

NOTES FOR BLOCKING:

PRODUCTION:

CINEMATOGRAPHY:

PRODUCTION DESIGN:

TO REMEMBER:

ADDITIONAL NOTES

OVERHEAD:

FILM TITLE:

Production company/ Director:

Date:	Scene #	INT/EXT	D/N	Shot #	Lens	Camera	Location	Sound

SHOT DESCRIPTION

SHOT

ELS LS MS AS CU ECU

ANGLE

MOVEMENT

NOTES FOR ACTORS:

NOTES FOR BLOCKING:

PRODUCTION:

CINEMATOGRAPHY:

PRODUCTION DESIGN:

TO REMEMBER:

ADDITIONAL NOTES

OVERHEAD:

FILM TITLE:

Production company/ Director:

Date:	Scene #	INT/EXT	D/N	Shot #	Lens	Camera	Location	Sound

SHOT DESCRIPTION

SHOT

ELS LS MS AS CU ECU

ANGLE

MOVEMENT

NOTES FOR ACTORS:

NOTES FOR BLOCKING:

PRODUCTION:

CINEMATOGRAPHY:

PRODUCTION DESIGN:

TO REMEMBER:

ADDITIONAL NOTES

OVERHEAD:

FILM TITLE:

Production company/ Director:

Date: | Scene # | INT/EXT | D/N | Shot # | Lens | Camera | Location | Sound

SHOT DESCRIPTION

SHOT: ELS | LS | MS | AS | CU | ECU

ANGLE

MOVEMENT

NOTES FOR ACTORS:

NOTES FOR BLOCKING:

PRODUCTION:

CINEMATOGRAPHY:

PRODUCTION DESIGN:

TO REMEMBER:

ADDITIONAL NOTES

OVERHEAD:

FILM TITLE:

Production company/ Director:

Date:	Scene #	INT/EXT	D/N	Shot #	Lens	Camera	Location	Sound

SHOT DESCRIPTION

SHOT

ELS LS MS AS CU ECU

ANGLE

MOVEMENT

NOTES FOR ACTORS:

NOTES FOR BLOCKING:

PRODUCTION:

CINEMATOGRAPHY:

PRODUCTION DESIGN:

TO REMEMBER:

ADDITIONAL NOTES

OVERHEAD:

FILM TITLE:

Production company/ Director:

Date:	Scene #	INT/EXT	D/N	Shot #	Lens	Camera	Location	Sound

SHOT DESCRIPTION

SHOT

ELS | LS | MS | AS | CU | ECU

ANGLE

MOVEMENT

NOTES FOR ACTORS:

NOTES FOR BLOCKING:

PRODUCTION:

CINEMATOGRAPHY:

PRODUCTION DESIGN:

TO REMEMBER:

ADDITIONAL NOTES

OVERHEAD:

FILM TITLE:

Production company/ Director:

Date:	Scene #	INT/EXT	D/N	Shot #	Lens	Camera	Location	Sound

SHOT DESCRIPTION

SHOT

ELS | LS | MS | AS | CU | ECU

ANGLE

MOVEMENT

NOTES FOR ACTORS:

NOTES FOR BLOCKING:

PRODUCTION:

CINEMATOGRAPHY:

PRODUCTION DESIGN:

TO REMEMBER:

ADDITIONAL NOTES

OVERHEAD:

FILM TITLE:

Production company/ Director:

Date:	Scene #	INT/EXT	D/N	Shot #	Lens	Camera	Location	Sound

SHOT DESCRIPTION

SHOT

ELS	LS	MS	AS	CU	ECU

ANGLE

MOVEMENT

NOTES FOR ACTORS:

NOTES FOR BLOCKING:

PRODUCTION:

CINEMATOGRAPHY:

PRODUCTION DESIGN:

TO REMEMBER:

ADDITIONAL NOTES

OVERHEAD:

FILM TITLE:

Production company/ Director:

Date:	Scene #	INT/EXT	D/N	Shot #	Lens	Camera	Location	Sound

SHOT DESCRIPTION

SHOT

ELS LS MS AS CU ECU

ANGLE

MOVEMENT

NOTES FOR ACTORS:

NOTES FOR BLOCKING:

PRODUCTION:

CINEMATOGRAPHY:

PRODUCTION DESIGN:

TO REMEMBER:

ADDITIONAL NOTES

OVERHEAD:

FILM TITLE:

Production company/ Director:

Date:	Scene #	INT/EXT	D/N	Shot #	Lens	Camera	Location	Sound

SHOT DESCRIPTION

SHOT

ELS | LS | MS | AS | CU | ECU

ANGLE

MOVEMENT

NOTES FOR ACTORS:

NOTES FOR BLOCKING:

PRODUCTION:

CINEMATOGRAPHY:

PRODUCTION DESIGN:

TO REMEMBER:

ADDITIONAL NOTES

OVERHEAD:

FILM TITLE:

Production company/ Director:

Date:	Scene #	INT/EXT	D/N	Shot #	Lens	Camera	Location	Sound

SHOT DESCRIPTION

SHOT

ELS LS MS AS CU ECU

ANGLE

MOVEMENT

NOTES FOR ACTORS:

NOTES FOR BLOCKING:

PRODUCTION:

CINEMATOGRAPHY:

PRODUCTION DESIGN:

TO REMEMBER:

ADDITIONAL NOTES

OVERHEAD:

FILM TITLE:

Production company/ Director:

Date:	Scene #	INT/EXT	D/N	Shot #	Lens	Camera	Location	Sound

SHOT DESCRIPTION

SHOT

ELS LS MS AS CU ECU

ANGLE

MOVEMENT

NOTES FOR ACTORS:

NOTES FOR BLOCKING:

PRODUCTION:

CINEMATOGRAPHY:

PRODUCTION DESIGN:

TO REMEMBER:

ADDITIONAL NOTES

OVERHEAD:

FILM TITLE:

Production company/ Director:

Date:	Scene #	INT/EXT	D/N	Shot #	Lens	Camera	Location	Sound

SHOT DESCRIPTION

SHOT

ELS LS MS AS CU ECU

ANGLE

MOVEMENT

NOTES FOR ACTORS:

NOTES FOR BLOCKING:

PRODUCTION:

CINEMATOGRAPHY:

PRODUCTION DESIGN:

TO REMEMBER:

ADDITIONAL NOTES

OVERHEAD:

FILM TITLE:

Production company/ Director:

Date:	Scene #	INT/EXT	D/N	Shot #	Lens	Camera	Location	Sound

SHOT DESCRIPTION

SHOT

ELS LS MS AS CU ECU

ANGLE

MOVEMENT

NOTES FOR ACTORS:

NOTES FOR BLOCKING:

PRODUCTION:

CINEMATOGRAPHY:

PRODUCTION DESIGN:

TO REMEMBER:

ADDITIONAL NOTES

OVERHEAD:

FILM TITLE:

Production company/ Director:

Date:	Scene #	INT/EXT	D/N	Shot #	Lens	Camera	Location	Sound

SHOT DESCRIPTION

SHOT

ELS LS MS AS CU ECU

ANGLE

MOVEMENT

NOTES FOR ACTORS:

NOTES FOR BLOCKING:

PRODUCTION:

CINEMATOGRAPHY:

PRODUCTION DESIGN:

TO REMEMBER:

ADDITIONAL NOTES

OVERHEAD:

FILM TITLE:

Production company/ Director:

Date:	Scene #	INT/EXT	D/N	Shot #	Lens	Camera	Location	Sound

SHOT DESCRIPTION

SHOT

ELS | LS | MS | AS | CU | ECU

ANGLE

MOVEMENT

NOTES FOR ACTORS:

NOTES FOR BLOCKING:

PRODUCTION:

CINEMATOGRAPHY:

PRODUCTION DESIGN:

TO REMEMBER:

ADDITIONAL NOTES

OVERHEAD:

FILM TITLE:

Production company/ Director:

Date:	Scene #	INT/EXT	D/N	Shot #	Lens	Camera	Location	Sound

SHOT DESCRIPTION

SHOT

ELS LS MS AS CU ECU

ANGLE

MOVEMENT

NOTES FOR ACTORS:

NOTES FOR BLOCKING:

PRODUCTION:

CINEMATOGRAPHY:

PRODUCTION DESIGN:

TO REMEMBER:

ADDITIONAL NOTES

OVERHEAD:

FILM TITLE:

Production company/ Director:

Date:	Scene #	INT/EXT	D/N	Shot #	Lens	Camera	Location	Sound

SHOT DESCRIPTION

SHOT

ELS LS MS AS CU ECU

ANGLE

MOVEMENT

NOTES FOR ACTORS:

NOTES FOR BLOCKING:

PRODUCTION:

CINEMATOGRAPHY:

PRODUCTION DESIGN:

TO REMEMBER:

ADDITIONAL NOTES

OVERHEAD:

FILM TITLE:

Production company/ Director:

Date:	Scene #	INT/EXT	D/N	Shot #	Lens	Camera	Location	Sound

SHOT DESCRIPTION

SHOT

ELS LS MS AS CU ECU

ANGLE

MOVEMENT

NOTES FOR ACTORS:

NOTES FOR BLOCKING:

PRODUCTION:

CINEMATOGRAPHY:

PRODUCTION DESIGN:

TO REMEMBER:

ADDITIONAL NOTES

OVERHEAD:

FILM TITLE:

Production company/ Director:

Date:	Scene #	INT/EXT	D/N	Shot #	Lens	Camera	Location	Sound

SHOT DESCRIPTION

SHOT

ELS LS MS AS CU ECU

ANGLE

MOVEMENT

NOTES FOR ACTORS:

NOTES FOR BLOCKING:

PRODUCTION:

CINEMATOGRAPHY:

PRODUCTION DESIGN:

TO REMEMBER:

ADDITIONAL NOTES

OVERHEAD:

FILM TITLE:

Production company/ Director:

Date:	Scene #	INT/EXT	D/N	Shot #	Lens	Camera	Location	Sound

SHOT DESCRIPTION

SHOT

ELS LS MS AS CU ECU

ANGLE

MOVEMENT

NOTES FOR ACTORS:

NOTES FOR BLOCKING:

PRODUCTION:

CINEMATOGRAPHY:

PRODUCTION DESIGN:

TO REMEMBER:

ADDITIONAL NOTES

OVERHEAD:

FILM TITLE:

Production company/ Director:

Date:	Scene #	INT/EXT	D/N	Shot #	Lens	Camera	Location	Sound

SHOT DESCRIPTION

SHOT

ELS LS MS AS CU ECU

ANGLE

MOVEMENT

NOTES FOR ACTORS:

NOTES FOR BLOCKING:

PRODUCTION:

CINEMATOGRAPHY:

PRODUCTION DESIGN:

TO REMEMBER:

ADDITIONAL NOTES

OVERHEAD:

FILM TITLE:

Production company/ Director:

Date:	Scene #	INT/EXT	D/N	Shot #	Lens	Camera	Location	Sound

SHOT DESCRIPTION

SHOT

ELS | LS | MS | AS | CU | ECU

ANGLE

MOVEMENT

NOTES FOR ACTORS:

NOTES FOR BLOCKING:

PRODUCTION:

CINEMATOGRAPHY:

PRODUCTION DESIGN:

TO REMEMBER:

ADDITIONAL NOTES

OVERHEAD:

FILM TITLE:

Production company/ Director:

Date:	Scene #	INT/EXT	D/N	Shot #	Lens	Camera	Location	Sound

SHOT DESCRIPTION

SHOT

ELS LS MS AS CU ECU

ANGLE

MOVEMENT

NOTES FOR ACTORS:

NOTES FOR BLOCKING:

PRODUCTION:

CINEMATOGRAPHY:

PRODUCTION DESIGN:

TO REMEMBER:

ADDITIONAL NOTES

OVERHEAD:

FILM TITLE:

Production company/ Director:

Date:	Scene #	INT/EXT	D/N	Shot #	Lens	Camera	Location	Sound

SHOT DESCRIPTION

SHOT

ELS | LS | MS | AS | CU | ECU

ANGLE

MOVEMENT

NOTES FOR ACTORS:

NOTES FOR BLOCKING:

PRODUCTION:

CINEMATOGRAPHY:

PRODUCTION DESIGN:

TO REMEMBER:

ADDITIONAL NOTES

OVERHEAD:

FILM TITLE:

Production company/ Director:

Date:	Scene #	INT/EXT	D/N	Shot #	Lens	Camera	Location	Sound

SHOT DESCRIPTION

SHOT

ELS | LS | MS | AS | CU | ECU

ANGLE

MOVEMENT

NOTES FOR ACTORS:

NOTES FOR BLOCKING.

PRODUCTION:

CINEMATOGRAPHY:

PRODUCTION DESIGN:

TO REMEMBER:

ADDITIONAL NOTES

OVERHEAD:

FILM TITLE:

Production company/ Director:

Date:	Scene #	INT/EXT	D/N	Shot #	Lens	Camera	Location	Sound

SHOT DESCRIPTION

SHOT						ANGLE	MOVEMENT
ELS	LS	MS	AS	CU	ECU		

NOTES FOR ACTORS:

NOTES FOR BLOCKING:

PRODUCTION:

CINEMATOGRAPHY:

PRODUCTION DESIGN:

TO REMEMBER:

ADDITIONAL NOTES

OVERHEAD:

FILM TITLE:

Production company/ Director:

Date:	Scene #	INT/EXT	D/N	Shot #	Lens	Camera	Location	Sound

SHOT DESCRIPTION

SHOT

ELS LS MS AS CU ECU

ANGLE

MOVEMENT

NOTES FOR ACTORS:

NOTES FOR BLOCKING:

PRODUCTION:

CINEMATOGRAPHY:

PRODUCTION DESIGN:

TO REMEMBER:

ADDITIONAL NOTES

OVERHEAD:

FILM TITLE:

Production company/ Director:

Date:	Scene #	INT/EXT	D/N	Shot #	Lens	Camera	Location	Sound

SHOT DESCRIPTION

SHOT

ELS LS MS AS CU ECU

ANGLE

MOVEMENT

NOTES FOR ACTORS:

NOTES FOR BLOCKING:

PRODUCTION:

CINEMATOGRAPHY:

PRODUCTION DESIGN:

TO REMEMBER:

ADDITIONAL NOTES

OVERHEAD:

FILM TITLE:

Production company/ Director:

Date:	Scene #	INT/EXT	D/N	Shot #	Lens	Camera	Location	Sound

SHOT DESCRIPTION

SHOT

ELS LS MS AS CU ECU

ANGLE

MOVEMENT

NOTES FOR ACTORS:

NOTES FOR BLOCKING:

PRODUCTION:

CINEMATOGRAPHY:

PRODUCTION DESIGN:

TO REMEMBER:

ADDITIONAL NOTES

OVERHEAD:

FILM TITLE:

Production company/ Director:

Date:	Scene #	INT/EXT	D/N	Shot #	Lens	Camera	Location	Sound

SHOT DESCRIPTION

SHOT

ELS LS MS AS CU ECU

ANGLE

MOVEMENT

NOTES FOR ACTORS:

NOTES FOR BLOCKING:

PRODUCTION:

CINEMATOGRAPHY:

PRODUCTION DESIGN:

TO REMEMBER:

ADDITIONAL NOTES

OVERHEAD:

FILM TITLE:

Production company/ Director:

Date:	Scene #	INT/EXT	D/N	Shot #	Lens	Camera	Location	Sound

SHOT DESCRIPTION

SHOT

ELS LS MS AS CU ECU

ANGLE

MOVEMENT

NOTES FOR ACTORS:

NOTES FOR BLOCKING:

PRODUCTION:

CINEMATOGRAPHY:

PRODUCTION DESIGN:

TO REMEMBER:

ADDITIONAL NOTES

OVERHEAD:

FILM TITLE:

Production company/ Director:

Date:	Scene #	INT/EXT	D/N	Shot #	Lens	Camera	Location	Sound

SHOT DESCRIPTION

SHOT

ELS | LS | MS | AS | CU | ECU

ANGLE

MOVEMENT

NOTES FOR ACTORS:

NOTES FOR BLOCKING:

PRODUCTION:

CINEMATOGRAPHY:

PRODUCTION DESIGN:

TO REMEMBER:

ADDITIONAL NOTES

OVERHEAD:

FILM TITLE:

Production company/ Director:

Date:	Scene #	INT/EXT	D/N	Shot #	Lens	Camera	Location	Sound

SHOT DESCRIPTION

SHOT

ELS LS MS AS CU ECU

ANGLE

MOVEMENT

NOTES FOR ACTORS:

NOTES FOR BLOCKING:

PRODUCTION:

CINEMATOGRAPHY:

PRODUCTION DESIGN:

TO REMEMBER:

ADDITIONAL NOTES

OVERHEAD:

FILM TITLE:

Production company/ Director:

Date:	Scene #	INT/EXT	D/N	Shot #	Lens	Camera	Location	Sound

SHOT DESCRIPTION

SHOT

ELS LS MS AS CU ECU

ANGLE

MOVEMENT

NOTES FOR ACTORS:

NOTES FOR BLOCKING:

PRODUCTION:

CINEMATOGRAPHY:

PRODUCTION DESIGN:

TO REMEMBER:

ADDITIONAL NOTES

OVERHEAD:

FILM TITLE:

Production company/ Director:

Date:	Scene #	INT/EXT	D/N	Shot #	Lens	Camera	Location	Sound

SHOT DESCRIPTION

SHOT

ELS LS MS AS CU ECU

ANGLE

MOVEMENT

NOTES FOR ACTORS:

NOTES FOR BLOCKING:

PRODUCTION:

CINEMATOGRAPHY:

PRODUCTION DESIGN:

TO REMEMBER:

ADDITIONAL NOTES

OVERHEAD:

FILM TITLE:

Production company/ Director:

Date:	Scene #	INT/EXT	D/N	Shot #	Lens	Camera	Location	Sound

SHOT DESCRIPTION

SHOT

ELS LS MS AS CU ECU

ANGLE

MOVEMENT

NOTES FOR ACTORS:

NOTES FOR BLOCKING:

PRODUCTION:

CINEMATOGRAPHY:

PRODUCTION DESIGN:

TO REMEMBER:

ADDITIONAL NOTES

OVERHEAD:

FILM TITLE:

Production company/ Director:

Date:	Scene #	INT/EXT	D/N	Shot #	Lens	Camera	Location	Sound

SHOT DESCRIPTION

SHOT

ELS | LS | MS | AS | CU | ECU

ANGLE

MOVEMENT

NOTES FOR ACTORS:

NOTES FOR BLOCKING:

PRODUCTION:

CINEMATOGRAPHY:

PRODUCTION DESIGN:

TO REMEMBER:

ADDITIONAL NOTES

OVERHEAD:

FILM TITLE:

Production company/ Director:

Date:	Scene #	INT/EXT	D/N	Shot #	Lens	Camera	Location	Sound

SHOT DESCRIPTION

SHOT

ELS LS MS AS CU ECU

ANGLE

MOVEMENT

NOTES FOR ACTORS:

NOTES FOR BLOCKING:

PRODUCTION:

CINEMATOGRAPHY:

PRODUCTION DESIGN:

TO REMEMBER:

ADDITIONAL NOTES

OVERHEAD:

FILM TITLE:

Production company/ Director:

Date:	Scene #	INT/EXT	D/N	Shot #	Lens	Camera	Location	Sound

SHOT DESCRIPTION

SHOT: ELS | LS | MS | AS | CU | ECU

ANGLE

MOVEMENT

NOTES FOR ACTORS:

NOTES FOR BLOCKING.

PRODUCTION:

CINEMATOGRAPHY:

PRODUCTION DESIGN:

TO REMEMBER:

ADDITIONAL NOTES

OVERHEAD:

FILM TITLE:

Production company/ Director:

Date:	Scene #	INT/EXT	D/N	Shot #	Lens	Camera	Location	Sound

SHOT DESCRIPTION

SHOT

ELS LS MS AS CU ECU

ANGLE

MOVEMENT

NOTES FOR ACTORS:

NOTES FOR BLOCKING:

PRODUCTION:

CINEMATOGRAPHY:

PRODUCTION DESIGN:

TO REMEMBER:

ADDITIONAL NOTES

OVERHEAD:

FILM TITLE:

Production company/ Director:

Date:	Scene #	INT/EXT	D/N	Shot #	Lens	Camera	Location	Sound

SHOT DESCRIPTION

SHOT

ELS LS MS AS CU ECU

ANGLE

MOVEMENT

NOTES FOR ACTORS:

NOTES FOR BLOCKING:

PRODUCTION:

CINEMATOGRAPHY:

PRODUCTION DESIGN:

TO REMEMBER:

ADDITIONAL NOTES

OVERHEAD:

FILM TITLE:

Production company/ Director:

Date:	Scene #	INT/EXT	D/N	Shot #	Lens	Camera	Location	Sound

SHOT DESCRIPTION

SHOT

ELS LS MS AS CU ECU

ANGLE

MOVEMENT

NOTES FOR ACTORS:

NOTES FOR BLOCKING:

PRODUCTION:

CINEMATOGRAPHY:

PRODUCTION DESIGN:

TO REMEMBER:

ADDITIONAL NOTES

OVERHEAD:

FILM TITLE:

Production company/ Director:

Date:	Scene #	INT/EXT	D/N	Shot #	Lens	Camera	Location	Sound

SHOT DESCRIPTION

SHOT

ELS LS MS AS CU ECU

ANGLE

MOVEMENT

NOTES FOR ACTORS:

NOTES FOR BLOCKING:

PRODUCTION:

CINEMATOGRAPHY:

PRODUCTION DESIGN:

TO REMEMBER:

ADDITIONAL NOTES

OVERHEAD:

FILM TITLE:

Production company/ Director:

Date:	Scene #	INT/EXT	D/N	Shot #	Lens	Camera	Location	Sound

SHOT DESCRIPTION

SHOT

ELS LS MS AS CU ECU

ANGLE

MOVEMENT

NOTES FOR ACTORS:

NOTES FOR BLOCKING:

PRODUCTION:

CINEMATOGRAPHY:

PRODUCTION DESIGN:

TO REMEMBER:

ADDITIONAL NOTES

OVERHEAD:

FILM TITLE:

Production company/ Director:

Date:	Scene #	INT/EXT	D/N	Shot #	Lens	Camera	Location	Sound

SHOT DESCRIPTION

SHOT

ELS LS MS AS CU ECU

ANGLE

MOVEMENT

NOTES FOR ACTORS:

NOTES FOR BLOCKING:

PRODUCTION:

CINEMATOGRAPHY:

PRODUCTION DESIGN:

TO REMEMBER:

ADDITIONAL NOTES

OVERHEAD:

FILM TITLE:

Production company/ Director:

Date:	Scene #	INT/EXT	D/N	Shot #	Lens	Camera	Location	Sound

SHOT DESCRIPTION

SHOT

ELS LS MS AS CU ECU

ANGLE

MOVEMENT

NOTES FOR ACTORS:

NOTES FOR BLOCKING:

PRODUCTION:

CINEMATOGRAPHY:

PRODUCTION DESIGN:

TO REMEMBER:

ADDITIONAL NOTES

OVERHEAD:

FILM TITLE:

Production company/ Director:

Date:	Scene #	INT/EXT	D/N	Shot #	Lens	Camera	Location	Sound

SHOT DESCRIPTION

SHOT

ELS LS MS AS CU ECU

ANGLE

MOVEMENT

NOTES FOR ACTORS:

NOTES FOR BLOCKING:

PRODUCTION:

CINEMATOGRAPHY:

PRODUCTION DESIGN:

TO REMEMBER:

ADDITIONAL NOTES

OVERHEAD:

FILM TITLE:

Production company/ Director:

Date:	Scene #	INT/EXT	D/N	Shot #	Lens	Camera	Location	Sound

SHOT DESCRIPTION

SHOT

ELS | LS | MS | AS | CU | ECU

ANGLE

MOVEMENT

NOTES FOR ACTORS:

NOTES FOR BLOCKING:

PRODUCTION:

CINEMATOGRAPHY:

PRODUCTION DESIGN:

TO REMEMBER:

ADDITIONAL NOTES

OVERHEAD:

FILM TITLE:

Production company/ Director:

Date:	Scene #	INT/EXT	D/N	Shot #	Lens	Camera	Location	Sound

SHOT DESCRIPTION

SHOT

ELS LS MS AS CU ECU

ANGLE

MOVEMENT

NOTES FOR ACTORS:

NOTES FOR BLOCKING:

PRODUCTION:

CINEMATOGRAPHY:

PRODUCTION DESIGN:

TO REMEMBER:

ADDITIONAL NOTES

OVERHEAD:

FILM TITLE:

Production company/ Director:

Date:	Scene #	INT/EXT	D/N	Shot #	Lens	Camera	Location	Sound

SHOT DESCRIPTION

SHOT

ELS LS MS AS CU ECU

ANGLE

MOVEMENT

NOTES FOR ACTORS:

NOTES FOR BLOCKING:

PRODUCTION:

CINEMATOGRAPHY:

PRODUCTION DESIGN:

TO REMEMBER:

ADDITIONAL NOTES

OVERHEAD:

FILM TITLE:

Production company/ Director:

Date:	Scene #	INT/EXT	D/N	Shot #	Lens	Camera	Location	Sound

SHOT DESCRIPTION

SHOT

ELS LS MS AS CU ECU

ANGLE

MOVEMENT

NOTES FOR ACTORS:

NOTES FOR BLOCKING:

PRODUCTION:

CINEMATOGRAPHY:

PRODUCTION DESIGN:

TO REMEMBER:

ADDITIONAL NOTES

OVERHEAD:

FILM TITLE:

Production company/ Director:

Date:	Scene #	INT/EXT	D/N	Shot #	Lens	Camera	Location	Sound

SHOT DESCRIPTION

SHOT

ELS LS MS AS CU ECU

ANGLE

MOVEMENT

NOTES FOR ACTORS:

NOTES FOR BLOCKING:

PRODUCTION:

CINEMATOGRAPHY:

PRODUCTION DESIGN:

TO REMEMBER:

ADDITIONAL NOTES

OVERHEAD:

FILM TITLE:

Production company/ Director:

Date:	Scene #	INT/EXT	D/N	Shot #	Lens	Camera	Location	Sound

SHOT DESCRIPTION

SHOT

ELS | LS | MS | AS | CU | ECU

ANGLE

MOVEMENT

NOTES FOR ACTORS:

NOTES FOR BLOCKING:

PRODUCTION:

CINEMATOGRAPHY:

PRODUCTION DESIGN:

TO REMEMBER:

ADDITIONAL NOTES

OVERHEAD:

FILM TITLE:

Production company/ Director:

Date:	Scene #	INT/EXT	D/N	Shot #	Lens	Camera	Location	Sound

SHOT DESCRIPTION

SHOT

ELS LS MS AS CU ECU

ANGLE

MOVEMENT

NOTES FOR ACTORS:

NOTES FOR BLOCKING:

PRODUCTION:

CINEMATOGRAPHY:

PRODUCTION DESIGN:

TO REMEMBER:

ADDITIONAL NOTES

OVERHEAD:

FILM TITLE:

Production company/ Director:

Date: Scene # INT/EXT D/N Shot # Lens Camera Location Sound

SHOT DESCRIPTION

SHOT ANGLE MOVEMENT

ELS LS MS AS CU ECU

NOTES FOR ACTORS:

NOTES FOR BLOCKING:

PRODUCTION:

CINEMATOGRAPHY:

PRODUCTION DESIGN:

TO REMEMBER:

ADDITIONAL NOTES

OVERHEAD:

FILM TITLE:

Production company/ Director:

Date:	Scene #	INT/EXT	D/N	Shot #	Lens	Camera	Location	Sound

SHOT DESCRIPTION

SHOT

ELS LS MS AS CU ECU

ANGLE

MOVEMENT

NOTES FOR ACTORS:

NOTES FOR BLOCKING:

PRODUCTION:

CINEMATOGRAPHY:

PRODUCTION DESIGN:

TO REMEMBER:

ADDITIONAL NOTES

OVERHEAD:

FILM TITLE:

Production company/ Director:

Date:	Scene #	INT/EXT	D/N	Shot #	Lens	Camera	Location	Sound

SHOT DESCRIPTION

SHOT

ELS LS MS AS CU ECU

ANGLE

MOVEMENT

NOTES FOR ACTORS:

NOTES FOR BLOCKING:

PRODUCTION:

CINEMATOGRAPHY:

PRODUCTION DESIGN:

TO REMEMBER:

ADDITIONAL NOTES

OVERHEAD:

FILM TITLE:

Production company/ Director:

Date:	Scene #	INT/EXT	D/N	Shot #	Lens	Camera	Location	Sound

SHOT DESCRIPTION

SHOT

ELS LS MS AS CU ECU

ANGLE

MOVEMENT

NOTES FOR ACTORS:

NOTES FOR BLOCKING:

PRODUCTION:

CINEMATOGRAPHY:

PRODUCTION DESIGN:

TO REMEMBER:

ADDITIONAL NOTES

OVERHEAD:

FILM TITLE:

Production company/ Director:

Date:	Scene #	INT/EXT	D/N	Shot #	Lens	Camera	Location	Sound

SHOT DESCRIPTION

SHOT

ELS LS MS AS CU ECU

ANGLE

MOVEMENT

NOTES FOR ACTORS:

NOTES FOR BLOCKING:

PRODUCTION:

CINEMATOGRAPHY:

PRODUCTION DESIGN:

TO REMEMBER:

ADDITIONAL NOTES

OVERHEAD:

FILM TITLE:

Production company/ Director:

Date:	Scene #	INT/EXT	D/N	Shot #	Lens	Camera	Location	Sound

SHOT DESCRIPTION

SHOT

ELS | LS | MS | AS | CU | ECU

ANGLE

MOVEMENT

NOTES FOR ACTORS:

NOTES FOR BLOCKING:

PRODUCTION:

CINEMATOGRAPHY:

PRODUCTION DESIGN:

TO REMEMBER:

ADDITIONAL NOTES

OVERHEAD:

FILM TITLE:

Production company/ Director:

Date:	Scene #	INT/EXT	D/N	Shot #	Lens	Camera	Location	Sound

SHOT DESCRIPTION

SHOT

ELS LS MS AS CU ECU

ANGLE

MOVEMENT

NOTES FOR ACTORS:

NOTES FOR BLOCKING:

PRODUCTION:

CINEMATOGRAPHY:

PRODUCTION DESIGN:

TO REMEMBER:

ADDITIONAL NOTES

OVERHEAD:

FILM TITLE:

Production company/ Director:

Date:	Scene #	INT/EXT	D/N	Shot #	Lens	Camera	Location	Sound

SHOT DESCRIPTION

SHOT

ELS LS MS AS CU ECU

ANGLE

MOVEMENT

NOTES FOR ACTORS:

NOTES FOR BLOCKING:

PRODUCTION:

CINEMATOGRAPHY:

PRODUCTION DESIGN:

TO REMEMBER:

ADDITIONAL NOTES

OVERHEAD:

FILM TITLE:

Production company/ Director:

Date:	Scene #	INT/EXT	D/N	Shot #	Lens	Camera	Location	Sound

SHOT DESCRIPTION

SHOT

ELS | LS | MS | AS | CU | ECU

ANGLE

MOVEMENT

NOTES FOR ACTORS:

NOTES FOR BLOCKING:

PRODUCTION:

CINEMATOGRAPHY:

PRODUCTION DESIGN:

TO REMEMBER:

ADDITIONAL NOTES

OVERHEAD:

FILM TITLE:

Production company/ Director:

Date:	Scene #	INT/EXT	D/N	Shot #	Lens	Camera	Location	Sound

SHOT DESCRIPTION

SHOT

ELS LS MS AS CU ECU

ANGLE

MOVEMENT

NOTES FOR ACTORS:

NOTES FOR BLOCKING:

PRODUCTION:

CINEMATOGRAPHY:

PRODUCTION DESIGN:

TO REMEMBER:

ADDITIONAL NOTES

OVERHEAD:

FILM TITLE:

Production company/ Director:

Date:	Scene #	INT/EXT	D/N	Shot #	Lens	Camera	Location	Sound

SHOT DESCRIPTION

SHOT

ELS | LS | MS | AS | CU | ECU

ANGLE

MOVEMENT

NOTES FOR ACTORS:

NOTES FOR BLOCKING:

PRODUCTION:

CINEMATOGRAPHY:

PRODUCTION DESIGN:

TO REMEMBER:

ADDITIONAL NOTES

OVERHEAD:

FILM TITLE:

Production company/ Director:

Date:	Scene #	INT/EXT	D/N	Shot #	Lens	Camera	Location	Sound

SHOT DESCRIPTION

SHOT

ELS LS MS AS CU ECU

ANGLE

MOVEMENT

NOTES FOR ACTORS:

NOTES FOR BLOCKING:

PRODUCTION:

CINEMATOGRAPHY:

PRODUCTION DESIGN:

TO REMEMBER:

ADDITIONAL NOTES

OVERHEAD:

FILM TITLE:

Production company/ Director:

Date:	Scene #	INT/EXT	D/N	Shot #	Lens	Camera	Location	Sound

SHOT DESCRIPTION

SHOT

ELS LS MS AS CU ECU

ANGLE

MOVEMENT

NOTES FOR ACTORS:

NOTES FOR BLOCKING:

PRODUCTION:

CINEMATOGRAPHY:

PRODUCTION DESIGN:

TO REMEMBER:

ADDITIONAL NOTES

OVERHEAD:

FILM TITLE:

Production company/ Director:

Date:	Scene #	INT/EXT	D/N	Shot #	Lens	Camera	Location	Sound

SHOT DESCRIPTION

SHOT

ELS LS MS AS CU ECU

ANGLE

MOVEMENT

NOTES FOR ACTORS:

NOTES FOR BLOCKING:

PRODUCTION:

CINEMATOGRAPHY:

PRODUCTION DESIGN:

TO REMEMBER:

ADDITIONAL NOTES

OVERHEAD:

FILM TITLE:

Production company/ Director:

Date:	Scene #	INT/EXT	D/N	Shot #	Lens	Camera	Location	Sound

SHOT DESCRIPTION

SHOT

ELS | LS | MS | AS | CU | ECU

ANGLE

MOVEMENT

NOTES FOR ACTORS:

NOTES FOR BLOCKING:

PRODUCTION:

CINEMATOGRAPHY:

PRODUCTION DESIGN:

TO REMEMBER:

ADDITIONAL NOTES

OVERHEAD:

FILM TITLE:

Production company/ Director:

Date:	Scene #	INT/EXT	D/N	Shot #	Lens	Camera	Location	Sound

SHOT DESCRIPTION

SHOT

ELS LS MS AS CU ECU

ANGLE

MOVEMENT

NOTES FOR ACTORS:

NOTES FOR BLOCKING:

PRODUCTION:

CINEMATOGRAPHY:

PRODUCTION DESIGN:

TO REMEMBER:

ADDITIONAL NOTES

OVERHEAD:

FILM TITLE:

Production company/ Director:

Date:	Scene #	INT/EXT	D/N	Shot #	Lens	Camera	Location	Sound

SHOT DESCRIPTION

SHOT

ELS LS MS AS CU ECU

ANGLE

MOVEMENT

NOTES FOR ACTORS:

NOTES FOR BLOCKING:

PRODUCTION:

CINEMATOGRAPHY:

PRODUCTION DESIGN:

TO REMEMBER:

ADDITIONAL NOTES

OVERHEAD:

FILM TITLE:

Production company/ Director:

Date:	Scene #	INT/EXT	D/N	Shot #	Lens	Camera	Location	Sound

SHOT DESCRIPTION

SHOT

ELS LS MS AS CU ECU

ANGLE

MOVEMENT

NOTES FOR ACTORS:

NOTES FOR BLOCKING:

PRODUCTION:

CINEMATOGRAPHY:

PRODUCTION DESIGN:

TO REMEMBER:

ADDITIONAL NOTES

OVERHEAD:

FILM TITLE:

Production company/ Director:

Date:	Scene #	INT/EXT	D/N	Shot #	Lens	Camera	Location	Sound

SHOT DESCRIPTION

SHOT

ELS LS MS AS CU ECU

ANGLE

MOVEMENT

NOTES FOR ACTORS:

NOTES FOR BLOCKING:

PRODUCTION:

CINEMATOGRAPHY:

PRODUCTION DESIGN:

TO REMEMBER:

ADDITIONAL NOTES

OVERHEAD:

FILM TITLE:

Production company/ Director:

Date:	Scene #	INT/EXT	D/N	Shot #	Lens	Camera	Location	Sound

SHOT DESCRIPTION

SHOT

ELS LS MS AS CU ECU

ANGLE

MOVEMENT

NOTES FOR ACTORS:

NOTES FOR BLOCKING:

PRODUCTION:

CINEMATOGRAPHY:

PRODUCTION DESIGN:

TO REMEMBER:

ADDITIONAL NOTES

OVERHEAD:

FILM TITLE:

Production company/ Director:

Date:	Scene #	INT/EXT	D/N	Shot #	Lens	Camera	Location	Sound

SHOT DESCRIPTION

SHOT

ELS LS MS AS CU ECU

ANGLE

MOVEMENT

NOTES FOR ACTORS:

NOTES FOR BLOCKING:

PRODUCTION:

CINEMATOGRAPHY:

PRODUCTION DESIGN:

TO REMEMBER:

ADDITIONAL NOTES

OVERHEAD:

FILM TITLE:

Production company/ Director:

Date:	Scene #	INT/EXT	D/N	Shot #	Lens	Camera	Location	Sound

SHOT DESCRIPTION

SHOT

ELS | LS | MS | AS | CU | ECU

ANGLE

MOVEMENT

NOTES FOR ACTORS:

NOTES FOR BLOCKING:

PRODUCTION:

CINEMATOGRAPHY:

PRODUCTION DESIGN:

TO REMEMBER:

ADDITIONAL NOTES

OVERHEAD:

FILM TITLE:

Production company/ Director:

Date:	Scene #	INT/EXT	D/N	Shot #	Lens	Camera	Location	Sound

SHOT DESCRIPTION

SHOT

ELS LS MS AS CU ECU

ANGLE

MOVEMENT

NOTES FOR ACTORS:

NOTES FOR BLOCKING:

PRODUCTION:

CINEMATOGRAPHY:

PRODUCTION DESIGN:

TO REMEMBER:

ADDITIONAL NOTES

OVERHEAD:

FILM TITLE:

Production company/ Director:

Date:	Scene #	INT/EXT	D/N	Shot #	Lens	Camera	Location	Sound

SHOT DESCRIPTION

SHOT: ELS | LS | MS | AS | CU | ECU

ANGLE

MOVEMENT

NOTES FOR ACTORS:

NOTES FOR BLOCKING:

PRODUCTION:

CINEMATOGRAPHY:

PRODUCTION DESIGN:

TO REMEMBER:

ADDITIONAL NOTES

OVERHEAD:

FILM TITLE:

Production company/ Director:

Date:	Scene #	INT/EXT	D/N	Shot #	Lens	Camera	Location	Sound

SHOT DESCRIPTION

SHOT

ELS | LS | MS | AS | CU | ECU

ANGLE

MOVEMENT

NOTES FOR ACTORS:

NOTES FOR BLOCKING:

PRODUCTION:

CINEMATOGRAPHY:

PRODUCTION DESIGN:

TO REMEMBER:

ADDITIONAL NOTES

OVERHEAD:

FILM TITLE:

Production company/ Director:

Date:	Scene #	INT/EXT	D/N	Shot #	Lens	Camera	Location	Sound

SHOT DESCRIPTION

SHOT

ELS | LS | MS | AS | CU | ECU

ANGLE

MOVEMENT

NOTES FOR ACTORS:

NOTES FOR BLOCKING:

PRODUCTION:

CINEMATOGRAPHY:

PRODUCTION DESIGN:

TO REMEMBER:

ADDITIONAL NOTES

OVERHEAD:

FILM TITLE:

Production company/ Director:

Date:	Scene #	INT/EXT	D/N	Shot #	Lens	Camera	Location	Sound

SHOT DESCRIPTION

SHOT

ELS LS MS AS CU ECU

ANGLE

MOVEMENT

NOTES FOR ACTORS:

NOTES FOR BLOCKING:

PRODUCTION:

CINEMATOGRAPHY:

PRODUCTION DESIGN:

TO REMEMBER:

ADDITIONAL NOTES

OVERHEAD:

FILM TITLE:

Production company/ Director:

Date:	Scene #	INT/EXT	D/N	Shot #	Lens	Camera	Location	Sound

SHOT DESCRIPTION

SHOT

ELS LS MS AS CU ECU

ANGLE

MOVEMENT

NOTES FOR ACTORS:

NOTES FOR BLOCKING:

PRODUCTION:

CINEMATOGRAPHY:

PRODUCTION DESIGN:

TO REMEMBER:

ADDITIONAL NOTES

OVERHEAD:

Manufactured by Amazon.ca
Bolton, ON